# Plan to Succeed

## The Workbook

## A Guide To Raising Business Capital

### by Al Stephen
### Greenfields Venture Capital

*This workbook is designed to assist you in the construction of your business plan and in the preparation of the successful presentation of your request for business capital.*

*PLAN TO SUCCEED – The Workbook*

# Businesses Need Capital

Successful businesses are well planned and well capitalized. Being well capitalized is having the ability to access capital when you need it. Being well planned will help you to be well capitalized. This workbook is designed to first help you become well planned and then lead you to becoming well capitalized.

I have watched many entrepreneurs lose valuable opportunities because they spent too much time negotiating with sources of funding who, at the end of the day, were not qualified. Just as in Sales you would qualify a prospect, so to in seeking capital. Speaking to qualified funders can prevent your window of opportunity passing you by. You should try to cut yourself a good deal, but the cost of capital should only be a consideration of the function of losses sustained by not having it.

Libraries and book stores are full of financial "How To Books" (I recommend you read as many as you can). These books will tell you about generic sources of capital, debt versus equity financing, business planning, goal setting, etc. This book will brush these topics, but its main focus is:

- What information to present to Lenders or Investors;
- How to package your request to get noticed;
- The format the presentation package should take; and,
- Where to find the Funding Source to provide the capital.
  *(If you don't know where to send your request, what's the point?)*

While there is no new technology discovered here, the methods are proven and you will surely benefit from using them. This book is designed to be a workbook. Get out your pencil and fill in each section as you go. Each chapter will guide you by asking you questions and giving you a place to arrive at your answers. When you are finished you will be able to remove the questions and your business plan will be complete, ready to submit to your potential funding sources.

The statistics show that 90% of all new businesses fail. Out of every ten new businesses, over a two year period, 3 will never fly, 3 will make a meager existence, 3 will slowly wither away and ONE will become a roaring success. I believe the failures are a direct result of failure to plan. Take the opportunity to plan and increase your chances of success.

### *"Failing to plan is planning to fail."*

### *Dream*      *<u>Scheme</u>*      *Team*

# *A Note From Experience*

### *"The man who believes he needs help from no one,*
### *quickly learns he has a fool for a partner."*

Being an Entrepreneur is not an easy endeavor.   Developing a business plan, requesting funding from strangers and facing the possibility of rejection makes it even harder.   Being an entrepreneur means taking risks, stepping out, endeavoring to make a difference, and getting up again when it all comes crashing down around your ears.

My adventures into business funding began with my own projects during the 1990's.   In the search for money I discovered literally hundreds of funding sources who couldn't help me.   I quickly learned that the world is full of agents; people who, entrepreneurial in their own right, seek to offer the services of investment companies who are not qualified to fund the business you are promoting.   Too much time running around talking to the wrong people means a window of opportunity (and the potential rewards) are lost forever.

During my experiences I have met and formed relationships with some of the most successful international business minds.   I have listened and I have learned and it is this knowledge that I hope will be effectively presented in this book.

I am constantly amazed at the infinite number of creative ways that entrepreneurs come up with for making money.   While you are out there becoming rich and famous (or poor and infamous), remember there is much more to life than making money.   And, I understand if sometimes it's hard to make sense of that statement !

My goal in writing this book is to make the process of finding capital easier for as many entrepreneurs as I possibly can.   I wish you the best of luck in your search for funding to achieve your goals, create jobs and promote free enterprise.

You will notice throughout this book that I like "quotes", some of them are funny and others are just great rules to help keep you on the right track.

Yours sincerely,

Al Stephen

### *"Even if you're on the right track,*
### *you'll get run over if you just sit there."*

**PLAN TO SUCCEED – The Workbook**

# Content Information

## Chapter

1. Plan for Success
   Executive Summary, History, Stage, Structure...

2. Players
   Ownership, Management, Consultants...

3. Strategic Position
   Nature of Market, Specific Niche...

4. Market Strategy
   Market penetration, market domination...

5. Setting Goals
   Every successful business has set goals...

6. Competition
   Why are you better, smarter, faster, cheaper...

7. Amount Requested
   Present a supported overview...

8. The Terms
   Know what you are looking for and can afford...

9. Use of Funds
   R&D, start-up costs, advertising, be specific...

10. Repayment Plan
    Massive sales, sell the business, go public...

11. Preparing Your Presentation
    The format and additional information...

12. Negotiating Your Deal
    First learn to say "No", then...

*"Nothing is quite so embarrassing as watching someone do what you told them couldn't be done."*

**PLAN TO SUCCEED – The Workbook**

# 1. *Plan For Success*

Capitalizing your business is a full time endeavor. Developing your business plan is the single most important step you can take toward your success. To maximize your potential to receive capital, it is *vital* that you develop a business plan that will guide your company and allow outsiders to picture where you are going and how you plan to get there. Take great care in preparing your plan, it is the road map that will lead you where you want to go. When you are finished the plan **PLEASE** don't be like so many others and put it on a shelf. Use, refine and improve it all the time. It will become the single most important tool you will have at your disposal for working "on" the business rather than "in" it. If you're one of the many who think you can do it without planning, then "Good Luck", you're going to need it. It amazes me that many people will plan and re-plan for a camping trip, but when they want to set up or buy a business they don't bother. Regardless of the reasons given, it is my belief that many don't plan because it's hard work. Creating an *effective* business is hard work. You are going to have to ask yourself a lot of soul searching questions and some of the answers might not be the ones you want to hear. If you don't ask the questions, the Bank Manager certainly will so it might be a good idea to have the answers ready when he asks.

Lenders or Investors, which way do I go? They tend to look at transactions from very different perspectives. Lenders are mostly concerned with "Can you repay?". While investors are more interested in "How far can you go?" There are certain items of information common to both. That will be the information to be disclosed at the start.

*"The Entrepreneur casts aside the assurance of forty hour weeks,*
*leaves the safe cover of tenure and security, and charges across*
*the perilous fields of change and opportunity.*

*If he succeeds, his reward will come not*
*from what he takes from his fellow man,*
*but from the value they freely place*
*on the gift of his imagination."*

# Executive Summary

This is it! Grab them here and you may never lose them. This summary is an overview description of your product or service, its market, your niche, the management, the mission, company structure, pro forma highlights, funding request, use of funds and proposed terms. No more than half a page, **sell the sizzle not the steak**. The summary is always written last, but appears first on the Business Plan.

**Narrative Section** Briefly describe what your company is all about. To assist you with this I include a number of key questions you can answer. Get as much information as possible but only put the brief highlights in the Executive Summary and cover the balance later in the plan.

1) What is your idea?
2) Why should customers buy the service and/or product?
3) What customer need does it meet?
4) Who are your potential customers?
5) What is the size of the market, now and in the future?
6) What competition do you face? If you say there isn't any there probably isn't a market!
7) Why is the product better than comparable alternatives?
8) What is innovative about your idea?
9) What is the value to the customer? Value is the single most important factor.
10) Can it make a profit? (And the answer is not just "YES"!)
11) What costs will be incurred before you show a profit?
12) What price will be asked?
13) How much money do you need?
14) Is the product/service legal? ie do you require any resource consents etc etc.
15) How do you plan to protect any intellectual property?
16) What stage of development has your idea reached?
17) What further steps do you plan to take?
18) What milestones must be reached?

## History

Your reader needs a summary of how this venture came to be. Where did the idea come from? How did it evolve? Who is responsible? Be concise but give dates, background, etc. Paint a short picture from how you started, to where you are today.

## Mission Statement

One sentence defining what the Company is all about. Think about it and *"make it mean something"*. Don't just write a bunch of flowery words. This should be "a call for you and your organisation to set, reach and maintain a standard of service, production, sales etc, etc".

*"The closest to perfection a person ever comes
is when they fill out their resume."*

**PLAN TO SUCCEED – The Workbook**

## Stage

Clearly identify what stage of funding you are at. Is your business a start-up, initial growth, positioning for going public, seeking a strategic partner, looking for near future acquisition or sale?

## Market Niche

It is important for any funding source to know where you fit in the economic food chain. What niche is your business exploiting that will make it jump over your competition? What are you doing that is better, faster, or newer than what everyone else is doing? For this part you must be very detailed. Remember the investors know nothing about your business. You must prove to them you know what you are doing or are about to do.

## Market Research

This is yours or a third parties research that supports your determination that there is a market and a need for your product or service. This will form the back bone of support for the price points and revenue assumptions contained in your pro forma projections indicating to investors or lenders how your company can turn a substantial profit.

## Financial Overview

Here is where you briefly highlight, graph and preview your outstanding financial projections. This provides a glimpse into where your gross sales, net income, net worth, etc. should be in years one , two and three. Remember this is only an overview. It should contain no details or support information. That will come later in your financial pro forma section.

# Write the Executive Summary last.

Give a brief yet concise explanation of the following items. Remember, you will fully detail and support each of these later on in your plan, so keep it short.

**Desired Amount:** _____

**Desired Terms:** _____

**Company Name:** _____

**Industry Type:** _____

**Time in Business:** _____

**Principals:** _____

**Use of Funds:** _____

**Collateral Offered:** _____

# 2. *Players*

Funding Sources are going to want to know with whom they are dealing. Important issues become; what are the qualifications, experience, goals and most of all the character of those in the management of this venture?

## Personal

Lenders and Investors are both concerned with whether or not you have what it takes to be successful. Highlight information that demonstrates you have the ability to make this business a success. Detail your education, past successes or failures that made you stronger. Indicate how you started this business and what makes you believe it will be a success.

## Character

Who are you? Take a deep look inside. Character is not only about winning. It's about getting up again and again when you've been knocked down. Will you panic in a crisis? Will you run for cover when things get rough? Are you the Captain that brings the ship in against all odds? Character is staying power! One of my favorite statements 'One man with courage is a majority' and it's true. If you have the courage and commitment and a 'never give up' attitude, you are a majority in yourself, and people with get the confidence you have in yourself.

To be a successful entrepreneur you must not only be able to start well, but you have to be able to finish strong. For most, running a business is a hard road and not an easy one. Search your soul. If you don't have this kind of character, do yourself and others a favor and don't even start.

## Management

Good management is essential. Funding Sources desire to see that you understand your market and have the skills to succeed. Are you a stand alone player, or are there others helping you? If alone, do you plan to keep it that way? Who will comprise your management team? Give detailed resumes of all those involved, along with a description of the vital roles they will play in the business' success. If your management skills or your team is weak, take on the task of building it up in order to support your own success, as well as the success of your funding request.

## Third Party Professionals

Listen to "GOOD" advice, and forget "BAD" counsel. Carefully seek out and select professionals who can help you. Do your homework in advance of your need to avoid delays. These legal, financial, tax, marketing, etc., professionals may be willing to advise your company for a piece of the glory to come or can act as consultants once you have the money to pay them. If you can't pay them immediately, be very clear and say so!! They may be willing to work out an arrangement.

## Survivorship

What plans have you made to ensure your business will continue to survive without you? Have you trained someone to take over? Is there going to be key man insurance in place for the possibility of illness, disability or death? Without you, can the business continue to survive? Describe how your management team will be able to step up and work the plan.

# 3. *Strategic Position*

Assume that your reader knows nothing. Even if you know they are experts, remember that the Lenders or Investors want to see that you know more about the industry and your market than they do.

### Market Overview

- General industry definition
- Current size and demand
- Potential target market
- Potential market growth
- Market share of competitors
- Technical evaluation of industry
- Direction of industry
- Current condition of industry

### Market Approach

- Initial plan to obtain a market share
- Resources available or allocated to market penetration
- Clearly defined long range market strategy
- Support assumptions on ability to hold market share

### Market Analysis

Who are the customers?

| | Percentage of Business |
|---|---|
| Private sector | _____ |
| Wholesalers | _____ |
| Retailers | _____ |
| Government | _____ |
| Other | _____ |

| We will target customers by: | |
|---|---|
| Product lines or services | _____ |
| Geographic area | _____ |
| Sales | _____ |

### *"At all times it is much better to have a plan."*

## Feasibility

Have you analyzed how successful your product or service can be?

What is the total potential market?

Is there really a market for you at all?

Does your company have the strength to get the job done?

Let outsiders know why this will work and be able to support what you believe in!

## Product Protection

What measures have you taken or will you take to insure the proprietary nature of your product? Patents, Trademarks, Copyrights, Trade Secrets, Proprietary Contracts, etc.

## Product or Service Analysis

If your product or service is of a proprietary nature, take steps to protect it. Have a non-disclosure/non-circumvention agreement for partners or investors to sign. Keep it simple. If it is too long or contains too many legal words, no one will sign it.

What is your product/service and what does it do?

What advantages does our product/service have over those of the competition?

What are the unique features, patents, expertise, etc.?

What disadvantages does your product or service have? (C'mon be honest!)

Where will you get your materials and supplies?

*"If you don't know what the customer value is,*
*the whole thing's a waste of time."*

**PLAN TO SUCCEED – The Workbook**

## Outside Factors

List the important economic factors that will affect your product or service. Consider things such as country growth, industry health, economic trends, rising prices, etc.:

What are the legal factors that will affect your market?

What are the government factors?

What factors, that you cannot control, will affect your market?

## Commercial Viability

Look for outside opinions on the commercial prospects of your product or service. There are numerous low cost or no cost organizations, such as retired executives or small business network groups to run your ideas by.

*"Business is like an automobile.*
*It won't run by itself, except downhill."*

# 4. *Market Strategy*

If you don't know where you are going and how you will get there, you are already lost.

## Market Position

What kind of image do you have?   Are you;   inexpensive, exclusive, customer service oriented, high quality, convenience, or fast?

List the features you will emphasize:

What pricing strategy will you use?

% Markup on cost     _____
Competitive     _____
Below competition     _____
Premium price     _____

Are your prices in line with your image?

What is the percentage of profit margin have you allowed for?

What customer services will you provide?

What are your sales/credit terms?

*" Marketing is far too important to be left to the Marketing Department. "*

## <u>Advertising/Promotion</u>

Write a short paragraph that best describes your business:


What advertising/promotion sources will you use?

Television      _____
Radio      _____
Direct mail      _____
Internet      _____
Magazines      _____
Newspaper      _____
Personal contacts      _____
Trade associations      _____
Yellow Pages      _____
Other      _____


What are the reasons you consider the chosen media to be the most effective?


What features will you promote?

Applications      _____
Price      _____
Performance      _____
Delivery      _____
Reputation      _____
Service      _____
Exclusivity      _____
Components      _____
Colors      _____
Sizes      _____
Uses      _____
Rugged      _____
Design      _____
Availability      _____
Installation      _____
Terms      _____
Workmanship      _____
Other      _____

*"Building a business is no small task. It will affect*
*all parts of your life, so consider well what you do."*

**PLAN TO SUCCEED – The Workbook**

What rationale will you appeal to?

| | |
|---|---|
| Accurate Performance | _____ |
| Increased Profits | _____ |
| Economy of Purchase | _____ |
| Increased Production | _____ |
| Durability | _____ |
| Labor Saving | _____ |
| Economy of Use | _____ |
| Time-Saving | _____ |
| Simple Construction | _____ |
| Simple Operation | _____ |
| Ease of Repair | _____ |
| Ease of Installation | _____ |
| Space Saving | _____ |
| Other | _____ |

What buying motive hot buttons will you use?

| | |
|---|---|
| Bigger Savings | _____ |
| Increased Sales | _____ |
| Greater Profits | _____ |
| Reduced Cost | _____ |
| Time Saved | _____ |
| Prestige | _____ |
| Greater Convenience | _____ |
| Uniform Production | _____ |
| Economy of Use | _____ |
| Reduced Upkeep | _____ |
| Continuous Output | _____ |
| Leadership | _____ |
| Ease of Use | _____ |
| Reduced Inventory | _____ |
| Low Operating Cost | _____ |
| Simplicity | _____ |
| Reduced Waste | _____ |
| Long Life | _____ |
| Other | _____ |

*"That's why many fail - they just don't get started -*
*they don't overcome the inertia of where they are -*
*they don't get going.*
*One of the hardness things to do is START."*

**PLAN TO SUCCEED – The Workbook**

What emotional responses can you use to your benefit?

Pride of Appearance      _____
Pride of Ownership       _____
Desire of Prestige        _____
Desire for Security       _____
Desire for Recognition   _____
Desire to Imitate         _____
Desire to be Unique     _____
Desire for Variety       _____
Fear                     _____
Desire to Create         _____
Convenience             _____
Curiosity               _____
Other                   _____

## Initial Market Penetration

How long will it take?

What capital resources will be required to acquire the initial share?

*"Doing business without advertising*
*is like winking at a girl in the dark,*
*you know what your doing, but nobody else does."*

# 5.  *Setting goals*

Having your short and long term goals set to paper is one attribute of all successful entrepreneurs.
## Benchmarks/Milestones

These are critical development stages the company has set to meet.   Without these visible and obtainable milestones your company and your investors may lose their way.   What are the first ten priority items to be accomplished as soon as your company gets the money?   How long should it take to complete them?

*Remember - A benchmark or milestone is - **a specific <u>measurable</u> result***

| | Priority | Time |
|---|---|---|
| 1. | _____ | _____ |
| 2. | _____ | _____ |
| 3. | _____ | _____ |
| 4. | _____ | _____ |
| 5. | _____ | _____ |
| 6. | _____ | _____ |
| 7. | _____ | _____ |
| 8. | _____ | _____ |
| 9. | _____ | _____ |
| 10. | _____ | _____ |

## Short Term

Near future…One year success points.   Define levels of your projected success that must be obtained in order to allow your pro forma to come true.   Set to paper obtainable goals that will show your investors how you plan to keep the company on track.

## Long Term

Lenders/Investors don't have your company vision.   Here is where you must paint a picture of the future for them.   This is the word version that supports what your pro forma has projected will take place over the next five years.

## Exit Strategy

Funding Sources want to know how you plan to pay them back.   Will the business generate a cash flow large enough to support the debt?   Is the product or service so in demand that the company will go public?   These questions and more will not only help determine your success, but they will also narrow your search for the lender most likely to fund your request.

## Personal

While your personal goals may not matter to your potential Lenders or Investors, they do matter to you and your company.   Deciding to be an entrepreneur can have great effects on your life and the lives of those around you.   Set down your personal goals just as you are writing this business plan.  Discuss them with your family.   Take the time to find out what your business associates expect of you.

# 6. *Competition*

Know your competition.   They can help you or bury you.

## Complementary Products

Show that you have searched out all those companies who offer competitive or related products.  Define those who offer complementary products in the same or similar industries.   Explain how competitive relationships can be turned into joint ventures, strategic partnerships, buyouts, acquisitions, etc. in the future. Lenders or Investors take comfort in the fact that you have defined possible exit solutions if things don't go as planned.

Who are your three major competitors?

Competitor #1 _____
Address          _____
                 _____

Years in Business      _____
Market Share           _____
Price/Strategy         _____
Product/Service        _____

Competitor #2 _____
Address          _____
                 _____

Years in Business      _____
Market Share           _____
Price/Strategy         _____
Product/Service        _____

Competitor #3 _____
Address          _____
                 _____

Years in Business      _____
Market Share           _____
Price/Strategy         _____
Product/Service        _____

*"If there isn't any competition there probably isn't a market."*

**Do a SWOT analysis - define your Strengths, Weaknesses, Opportunities and Threats -** Compare your strengths and weaknesses to your competition's.  Consider such things as location, size of resources, reputation, services, personnel, etc.

**Strengths:**                                             **Weaknesses:**

**Opportunities:**                                          **Threats:**

## Current Market Share

It is vital that you demonstrate an expert understanding of what your industry is all about.  Where is your industry going?

What is the current condition of your industry?

Why are the current market distributions the way they are?

What has your competition done to achieve their market share?

What advertising media is most effectively used by your competition?

## Trade Associations

Give a reference to all trade associations that cover your industry.  Use material supplied by these organizations to support statements and assumptions you have made throughout your funding request.

List the trade associations that service your industry:

*"Efficient executives find machines that can do half their work, and then buy two."*

# 7. *Amount Requested*

## Conservative Request

It is extremely important that your financial projections fully support the amount of funds you are seeking. If you are seeking debt financing your request must be very specific. Lenders frown upon you having to come back to ask for more, because you underestimated. Investors may not be inclined to keep your management team in place if you can't make the funding work.

## Downside Planning

Take the time to plan for the downside. It is far better to over estimate your capital requirements than to run short and be forced to go hat in hand back for more. Investors will not bankroll your business. ask for how much you need first off, taking into account the downside. Remember, if you have to go back for more, you've probably blown it with your investor and he will look to exercise the escape clause.

## Supportable Assumptions

Both Lenders and Investors are going to want to know that you have reasonably estimated and supported your costs and projected revenues. Your financial pro forma should include detailed information and trade references on the costs of each expense you list.

## Association Documentation

In your income projections be sure to include Trade Industry support information or other market information that lends credibility to the conclusions you have drawn. Most associations publish reports of standard industry costs, margins and financial ratios.

*"It is especially hard to work for money that you've already spent, on something that you didn't need."*

# 8. *The Terms*

Know what you want, what you can afford and what you will give up.

## How Long?

This should be based on your financial pro forma or the useful life of the asset being financed. Receivable and contract financing are less than 12 months, equipment normally one to five years, real estate and other long term assets 5 to 20 years.

## Amortized versus Interest Only

Most ventures take some time to begin making money. New equipment or other acquired assets take time to begin paying for themselves. Think about an initial period of interest only or skip payments to offset your lack of cash flow.

## Interest Rate

The rate you pay for the funds you need can directly affect your profitability. On the other hand, if by paying 50% interest, you yield 100% profitability, you are way ahead of where you began.

## Fixed or Adjustable

With a fixed rate of interest you know where you are. With adjustable rates you're betting on the future. Rates vary as you add or subtract risk.

## Points and Fees

Most, if not all, funding sources charge points (percentage of amount funded) and fees (costs of putting your transaction together). These can run from 1% to 10% depending on what you're looking for and the degree of risk. Fees are sometimes payable 50% at commitment and 50% at closing. Try to get 100% at closing or at least deposit the 50% into a trust or escrow account. Beware of those sources who must have your money before you see theirs'.

## Prepayment Penalties

Funding sources spend time, energy and money picking deals to invest in. Once they lend or invest they want to stick with it. Pre-payment penalties are one way to insure you'll leave the funds in place. Try to negotiate these away, or limit them to one or two years.

## Blanket & Specific Liens (Collateral)

Blanket means "all". Specific is just that. Blanket liens will restrict your ability to raise cash in the future. Always attempt to have specific liens.

## Personal Guarantees

How committed are you? If you won't sign personally, then you may not get any money. This is a gut check. If you don't believe in your success, why should anyone else? As you and your company perform, you should be able to get these released.

## Covenants & Conditions

Be very careful. These spell out just what you can and cannot do. No management or ownership change, quarterly filing requirements, no borrowing from anyone else, deposits maintained, collateral pledges, etc. Read and evaluate the fine print.

## % Ownership You Will Offer

What's fair? 80%, 50%, 20%... I can't tell you. You must define it, support it, and defend it. While most lenders won't ask, most investors will demand. Be prepared from the start. Do your homework on your potential funding sources.

## Stock Repurchase Agreement?

What happens if you hate your investor? Are you locked together forever? Try to negotiate escape clauses that will allow you a way out if you need it or can afford it. Be able to buy your stock back at a predetermined price, if possible.

## Management Controls?

Most entrepreneurs are in business to make decisions for themselves. Some investors want almost a partnership. Once again, pre-plan and know what you are looking for and what you are willing to give up.

## Collateral Anyone?

Will you risk it all? If you don't believe, neither will anyone else.
- Accounts Receivable
- Contracts
- Equipment
- Inventory
- Marketable Securities
- Purchase Orders
- Real Estate
- OP (Other Peoples )

*"No business opportunity is ever lost.*
*If you lose it, your competitor will find it."*

**PLAN TO SUCCEED – The Workbook**

# 9. *Use of Funds*

Entrepreneurs tend to spend too much time looking for money and not enough time making money.   This problem stems from the lack of adequate pre-planning given to the initial use of funds.   In order to determine what your short and long term capital needs are going to be, you must perform accurate financial projections.

Those projections must consider:

- Immediate Need For Capital (Bills to pay)

- Research and Development (Estimate, then double)

- Capital Asset Acquisition (Required equipment, etc.)

- Inventory Floor Planning (Necessary raw materials)

- Working Capital Requirements (Payroll, payables, etc.)

- Market Penetration (When will the cash flow begin)

The cash flow model is the best tool for determining what your capital needs will be.   Don't be overly optimistic or conservative, either one will hurt you.   Know what factors will affect your projections to the downside, (sales, costs, price breaks, etc.).   Work closely with third parties, financial advisors, accountants, industry consultants, retired executives, etc., to keep from having tunnel vision and missing the big picture. Your cash flow model should be month to month for one year and quarterly for the next four years.

*"Anyone who thinks the customer isn't right,
should try doing without them for ninety days."*

# 10. *Repayment Plan*

Repayment is tied directly to your success.    In order to repay your Funding Source, you must clearly define how you are going to make money and how much money you are going to make.

## R&D Requirements

How much research and development remains before you can enter the market?  Does your product require regulatory approval?  What is your time table?  What delays are foreseeable that could affect your time table? Are there any alternative plans if tests, approvals, patents, licenses, etc., don't go as planned?

## Break Even Analysis

Exactly where is it?  Must you sell 10,000 widgets?  How will price breaks effect you?  Can your salespeople survive on your commission structure?  What about material price increases?  Here is where you are going to demonstrate that you understand your product, its market, its costs and your industry.

## Current or Projected Debt Coverage Ratio

*Remember 1.25 to 1.* It's a figure that can affect your future.  For lenders if your net income is below 1.25 to 1, it may mean no loan, a higher rate or more collateral.  Simply put, it determines your ability to service debt.  Your net income should be 1.25 times higher than the debt payment you are proposing to take on. Hopefully you have analyzed your debt coverage ratio and found it to be much higher.  If it's not, this leaves a pretty slim margin for error.

With investors, because there is no debt, they are concerned with profit margins and retained earnings.  The projections should support ratios of better than 2.0 to 1 to generate any serious investor interest.

## Amortization or Dividend

- Return on investment
- Return of investment

These are terms that all funding sources want to know.   If they give you the money, what do you project your time table to be for them to get their investment back?   Then, when does the return on the investment start?

*"I can't be out of money, I still have cheques."*

# 11. *Preparing Your Presentation*

Take great care in your preparation of all the items mentioned in chapters 1 through 11 of this book. Unfortunately, you normally only get one shot per funding source, so make it your best!

## Have Additional Information Packaged and Ready

- Schedule of Assets
- Personal Financial Statements
- Credit Report Releases
- Business Tax Returns
- Personal Tax Returns
- Articles of Incorporation
- Copies of Orders or Invoices
- Customer Testimonials
- Trade References
- Banking References
- Title Reports (equipment, real estate, etc.)
- Asset Appraisals
- Patents, Trademarks or Licenses

## Presentation

- First impressions are lasting, make a good one.
- Use a color product brochure as a cover.
- Bind the material so that it opens flat on the table and allows for easy reading.
- Tab each section for direct access.
- Keep your information concise and to the point.
- Pictures are worth a thousand words, include good ones.
- Support assumptions with facts, not more assumptions.

### *"Reality forms around a commitment."*

# 12. *Negotiating Your Deal*

First learn to say **NO**. Now you're ready to negotiate. Most Entrepreneurs approach the issue of negotiating with great stress and anxiety. This leads directly to weak negotiations or becoming defensive about being asked too many questions. Either way, you lose! In order to avoid this happening to you, please go back to chapter eight "Terms" and make sure you have clearly defined what you are looking for before the negotiations begin. Then…

- Determine which points are worth fighting for.
- Express your objections and questions to any point.
- Get it in writing, leave **nothing** to verbal agreements.
- Subject everything to your long range goals.
- Pay close attention to what triggers default and what actions may be taken in this event.
- Establish ceilings and caps. You don't want to be stuck paying huge payments if rates go up. Avoid ratchet clauses like the plague.
- Get it in writing, leave **nothing** to verbal agreements.
- Plan for the downside. Attempt to have an "interest only" clause or "skip payment" provision in the event of slow downs.
- Look for no pre-payment penalty or the right to buy back your stock at a fixed price.
- Pay attention to covenants, conditions, ratios, restrictions or other clauses which can have serious long term effects.
- Get it in writing, leave **nothing** to verbal agreements.
- Try to minimize pledging collateral. You may need those assets in the future to raise additional capital.
- Seek professional counsel before you sign anything. Lawyers and accountants may not help you fund your deal, but they can help you spot the small details that may burden you down the road, and finally,
- Get it in writing, leave **nothing** to verbal agreements!

Seriously, if it is worth saying it is worth putting on paper. You can bank on nothing that isn't on paper.

*"Business is the art of extracting money from another
person's pocket without resorting to violence."*

## Close

This is a good place to do just that.   Remember you are out there selling yourself and your company.  Be a closer!  Only accept "No",  as being one step nearer to **"Yes"**.  I hope the material presented here will help you plan for your success and locate the funding that every business needs.

> *" I cannot give you a formula for success,*
> *but I can give you the formula for failure:*
> *Be one of those who think they have it all in their head ."*

If there is one thing I can say that will assist greatly in your success it is this,

### *" START "*

this means write it down, putting your thoughts to paper crystallizes them and allows you to develop your thoughts into a plan - your business plan.

Your plan is a "call to be in action".

## Knowledge  +  Action  =  Results

$$\frac{\text{People  +  Service}}{\text{Product}} \quad \rightarrow \quad \text{Profit}$$

Good luck in your search for funding!